DON'T LET CHALLENGES GET THE BEST OF YOU

DON'T LET CHALLENGES GET THE BEST OF YOU

Turning negative situations into positive solutions

BENIGNO A. ROMAN

Printed in the United States of America.

ISBN: 978-0-578-83672-0

For information contact:
E-mail: overcomelifechallenges100@gmail.com

Library of Congress Cataloging-in-Publication Data

This book is dedicated to my late grandmother. She was a hardworking person with a beautiful spirit. I'm grateful for the love she shared and the wonderful memories we made together. It takes an extraordinary person to go above and beyond for another individual.

TABLE OF CONTENTS

ACKNOWLEDGMENTS

My father and aunt encouraged me to write this book. I cannot thank you both enough. I'm grateful for your suggestions, opinions, and most of all, your support. Thank you for helping me turn a goal into a reality.

INTRODUCTION

I wrote this book to tell my life story and to encourage young people dealing with similar circumstances. As I describe my journey from childhood to early adulthood, I also offer insight, explaining how I overcame the challenges I faced along the way. The final chapter offers advice on how to triumph over adversity — a topic I have learned a great deal about.

My only ask is this: after reading my story, reflect on your own. Think about how you can use some of these suggestions in your life. I hope that you remember to never give up, no matter how many obstacles are thrown your way.

CHAPTER ONE

Infancy to Early Childhood

I cannot describe the first years of my life without describing the people who significantly influenced it. I was born prematurely to my mother in Queens, New York, and immediately released to my grandmother. My mother had a substance abuse problem and my grandmother raised me, my brother, and one of my younger sisters from birth. I longed for my mother – all of us did. But to be honest, being raised by my grandmother was one of the best things that ever happened to me.

My grandmother showed me enough love for a lifetime and raised me as her own child. I called her "grandma" but we actually weren't blood related — she was my brother's biological grandmother and he and I have different fathers. Nevertheless, she did everything in her power to make sure I was comfortable. She spoiled me rotten. I grew up in a large, two-bedroom, two-bathroom apartment with a terrace. It was magnificent. She didn't earn a lot of money, but she was decorative — her living room was filled with glass ornaments and plants. She kept the place spotless, always washing clothes and dishes, ironing, and cooking meals. And man, did she cook. It was her passion and you could taste it in every bite. She always cooked breakfast, lunch, and dinner, making everything from soul food to cakes and pies.

For me, it wasn't just about the living space my grandmother created — it was about the life she lived and the example she set. She was an outspoken woman — loud and straight to the point. She was stern but lenient. She was strong and independent. She nurtured me and loved me with her entire being. She was my first love and one of the most influential people in my life.

One of the other critical people in my life at the time was my brother. He was my big brother — five years older and the polar opposite of me. He was tough and outgoing. I was laid back and serious. He was tall and built. I was short and chubby. He was slim and trim and always active in sports. He was also always great at getting girls. My brother was taught to look after me and I learned to look up to him. He was like my bodyguard. He made sure that no one messed with me and I always admired that about him.

As we grew older, our relationship grew distant. My brother got involved in crime and got in trouble with the law. He was arrested a few times and became more violent. I remember him getting involved in a knife fight with an older teenage boy. The older teenager was left severely injured and my brother also suffered injuries. As time went on, he was involved in more and more incidents like this. He got arrested for one thing after another. He joined a notorious gang, the Bloods. My grandmother tried her best to get my brother on a better path, but he didn't want to hear it and eventually moved out. He went to live with my mother in Harlem.

At the time, my mother was putting her life back together. She was sober and wasn't using drugs. She rented a three-bedroom apartment and had a decent paying job as a nursing assistant at Bellevue Hospital. I was happy for her — she always wanted to work in nursing.

My mother felt guilty about her drug history, so she was lenient with my brother. Too lenient. He did whatever he wanted in her house – smoked weed, used drugs, and drank. It became clear to all of us that my brother was heading down the wrong path.

CHAPTER TWO

Childhood

When I was nine years old, one weekend changed my life. I went to my grandmother's house, and I remember her whispering in my ear, "Your father is coming to get you. You're going to live with him." I didn't know what was going on, but I knew I didn't like that. When my father arrived at my grandmother's house, I didn't want to leave. He had to pick me up and physically remove me. I was yelling and screaming, "I want to live with Grandma!" It was an emotional experience for me.

I lived with my father for about a year and a half. It was a challenging time. I was forced to live in a new environment, surrounded by new people, and exposed to a new way of parenting. My father believed in tough love — he was not one to spoil a child. He spent most of his time working and was in a relationship with a woman who was not my mother. How did I respond to this change? I rebelled. I was accustomed to my grandmother's way of doing things. My father hated that. He always pushed me to be more disciplined.

On one occasion, I lied to my father about hiding my cousin's bookbag. When my father found out, he whipped my ass with a belt. When I got older, I realized that parents, in general, don't want to whip their children. Sometimes it's necessary when a child is uncontrollable or misbehaving. But at the time, I was shocked. I had never experienced a whipping before. The belt left marks on my skin. I told my grandmother what happened and she told me to tell my teachers. An investigation was opened, Child Services was called, and eventually, my mother was given full custody. I went to live with her and my brother in Harlem.

To be honest, I enjoyed living with my mother at this time. It was the first time that all of my siblings had lived together and we all developed a bond. We went to church every Sunday and still saw my grandmother regularly — she was helping us financially and of course, still providing her love. One of my favorite memories from this time was performing in a talent show with my mom — it was just the two of us. We sang, "You Are Not Alone," by Michael Jackson. It was a special moment for both of us.

CHAPTER THREE

Adolescence

When I was eleven, my mother moved our family to South Carolina. Her mother was dying of cancer, and once she passed, my mother assumed ownership of her home. In all honestly, the death of my mother's mother didn't affect me because I never had a relationship with her. What did affect me was the move, and the impact the move had on my mother. Once she was back in the South, she reconnected with old friends and family members who didn't have her best interests at heart. She began drinking. I can distinctly remember one day when she was drinking while driving me around. Her attitude changed and she started venting and talking loudly. She became aggressive. It was the first time I had seen my mother under the influence of alcohol, but unfortunately, it wouldn't be the last.

As my mother spiraled further into her drinking habits, I worked hard to hold our family together. I didn't have a choice. I was both a brother and a parental figure to my two younger sisters. I made sure they were always fed and on time for school. At the same time, I was a student in junior high school and had to work hard to keep my grades up. It was a lot to handle and more than someone my age should have been forced to deal with.

Meanwhile, my mother spent her time drinking, partying, and hanging out with folks who were bad influences. She came home intoxicated almost every day. One night, things escalated when my mother came home drinking and fussing with my brother and I. My mother called the cops and they came, guns were drawn. My brother was sitting on a couch, arguing with the officers. They were trying to get him to stand up and walk out the door. He was mouthing off with a huge pillow covering his arms. I was terrified — I didn't know if they would start shooting. After all, they couldn't see his hands. Finally, my brother threw the pillow on the floor and walked outside. They arrested him, but I don't even remember why.

As more time passed, my mother continued drinking. It was her new norm. Initially, her drink of choice was beer; then it became liquor. It became clear to me that most of my mother's problems stemmed from her alcohol addiction and dating choices. She was always drawn to no good men. Don't get me wrong, she had plenty of opportunities to be with men who cared for her, but she never treated them right. My favorite was Calvin. He was from New York and moved to South Carolina to live with my mother. He wanted to help her and take care of us. He made the best fried chicken. No, he wasn't perfect, but he wanted to be there for our family and to love my mother. Then my mother spat in his face during another drunken outburst. That was that — we never saw Calvin again.

Soon after, I reached a breaking point. My mother came home late one night, intoxicated and fussing at me about something insignificant. She cursed me out and scratched up my face. The verbal and physical abuse was both shocking and devastating. This wasn't the mother I remembered. I was deeply hurt and emotionally wounded. I felt overwhelmed with pain. I called the only person I could trust: my grandmother. When she answered the phone, I said, "Grandma, please help me." I told her I couldn't take it anymore. She said, "Okay baby, I'm coming to get you right after you graduate from junior high school." I was overjoyed — that was only a few months away. Each day after that event felt like an eternity. When my graduation day finally arrived, my mother was drunk once again. I barely cared. All I could think about was the fact that graduating meant I was moving on with my life. I no longer had to live in South Carolina.

When my grandmother came to pick me up, I met her at a Greyhound bus station. I was so happy to see her. We took a cab to my mother's house. I didn't tell my mother she was coming, so of course, my mother tried to pick a fight. I got in the middle of it — I refused to let her place a finger on my grandmother. My mother ended up scratching my face up again. I knew it was time to leave. My grandmother and I went to my brother's house where she cooked a delicious meal for all of us. She made all of my childhood favorites. We left the next day.

Even though I was desperate to leave South Carolina, actually doing so was hard. I left my sisters who were my world at the time. I also left my first girlfriend, which was tough because we had become close. We tried a long-distance relationship, but it didn't work out.

Living in New York presented a new set of challenges. I was extremely lonely. So when my brother surprised me by visiting with his girlfriend and child, I was happy — I knew that for a few days, I wouldn't be alone. But that happiness was short-lived. One day, my brother and I got into a heated argument. Things almost got physical, but my grandmother intervened by separating us into different rooms. She called my father to help her with the situation. My father took in my brother and his family for a while. However, he soon found out my brother was selling drugs and kicked him out. With no job and no clear direction, my brother went back to South Carolina, where he got arrested — again.

A bright spot came in June of 2008 when I graduated from the High School for Arts and Business in Queens, New York. Having been through a lot by that point, it was a huge achievement for me. I remember feeling all of the love from those who came to support me that day – my grandmother, parents, sisters, a friend, and two of my cousins. I also remember celebrating by downing several stacks of pancakes at IHOP later that day.

I was officially my own man — 18 and ready to take on the world. Unfortunately, my world would be shaken yet again because of the negative interactions with my brother's father. My grandmother's son lived in her home with us, and he was an older adult who was jealous of our relationship. He craved attention and hated the fact that she adored me. He despised our close bond. He wanted everything that I had and he even tried to fight me. My father always knew my grandmother's son was jealous of me. He later explained that the only reason he had me stay in her house was so that I could develop a relationship with my brother. He knew he would never win custody of my brother so he decided to keep me there where we would be together. However, when my father got word that my grandmother's son had a loaded gun in the house, he knew he had to act fast to keep me safe.

Eventually, my father and I moved in together, renting a two-bedroom apartment in East New York. We only lived there for six months, but it was the first time I lived in the projects. The neighborhood was terrible and the lifestyle was unbearable. People urinated in the elevator. I walked outside and saw my neighbor beating his lady to the ground. I remember feeling shocked at that moment — I had never seen a woman be so badly beaten. One of the neighbors told me, "You'll get used to it." But I knew I never would — I would never get used to living like an animal.

Although living in the projects with my father was challenging, we formed a close bond. He was unable to work at the time, but he did have a stable income. Honestly, I benefited from having him home — we had plenty of time to talk and realize how much we had in common.

Our conversations were always deep. He learned about my challenges and I learned about his. To this day, I attribute our close relationship to the time we spent together in the projects. I know that I can always express my true feelings and talk to him about anything.

In October of 2009, my father and I moved to a luxury building in midtown Manhattan. Coming from the projects, it felt like living in a different world. We enjoyed all the amenities, but the downside was the size — it was a one-bedroom apartment. I knew that eventually; I'd have to move out and leave my father.

CHAPTER FOUR

Early Adulthood

After high school, I attended Queensborough Community College where I majored in liberal arts and science (I wasn't exactly sure about my career path at the time). Eventually, I selected a field of study that felt right for me — criminal justice. I had always been interested in the justice system. I transferred to John Jay College of Criminal Justice and planned to obtain a law enforcement position and later pursue teaching. I graduated from the school in 2013, earning my bachelor's degree.

I got my first taste of working in law enforcement in January of 2012 when I accepted a position as an Urban Park Ranger for the New York City Department of Parks and Recreation. I graduated from the Urban Park Ranger Academy and learned a great deal about the true duties of a law enforcement officer. Unfortunately, the department had limited opportunities for advancement, and salaries in my division were low. I resigned, hoping to find a position at a larger agency with more opportunities.

Around the same time, I rented my first apartment — a studio in the Eastchester Heights region of the Bronx. I quickly learned that I had made a big mistake. The neighborhood was a disaster and completely unsafe. I was almost robbed the day I moved in. I remember lying in my bed when I realized someone was trying to use a butterknife to pick the lock of my front door. I was able to block the door with my body and eventually, the would-be intruders gave up. My father came and changed the locks on my door the next day. This experience taught me a few things. I learned to do extensive research on a neighborhood before moving in. I also learned to visit a community at night and during the day. Perhaps most importantly, I realized I didn't want to be a renter. I vowed that I would own the next place I lived in.

In September of 2012, I began working as a coach cleaner for a large commuter railroad company. I was employed in this position for eight years and I worked hard every single day. It was tough. I cleaned up after hundreds of customers who seemingly had no regard for cleanliness. I encountered coffee stains, beer spills, newspapers, and loads of beer bottles. Some of the trains smelled horrible. Customers often vomited inside the cars. Passengers left feces on bathroom walls and bloodstains on seats. I even worked as a dumper — the person who is responsible for removing waste from the toilets.

I tried to get promoted within the company and submitted applications for various positions. I accepted the position with the understanding that advancement would be easier since I was already an employee. That belief proved to be false.

I did learn from this experience, however. I learned not to judge a job based on the salary attached to it. I also learned that you complete a job minute by minute, and a minute can feel like an eternity if you're in the wrong position.

The railroad job had been a disappointment, but it did allow me to save money. In June of 2013, I proudly bought my first co-op apartment in Laurelton, Queens, New York. I was twenty-two at the time. It felt good to own my apartment. It was located in a beautiful, quiet neighborhood. My neighbors were peaceful and friendly. I even had the luxury of having my mentor help me fix up the property and get it to my liking. He was able to fix nearly anything. While I loved owning the place, it wasn't perfect — I could hear everything my neighbors did and did not like the fact that the space was so small. I sold it after living there for seven years, but I never lost the pride I felt in working so hard to reach my ownership goal.

In August of 2015, I experienced unforgettable heartbreak. I lost my grandmother — she passed due to complications from a knee replacement surgery. She had been having pain in her knee that made it difficult to walk. She checked herself into a hospital where the doctor gave her something she was allergic to. Her body did not respond well and she never recovered. It was the saddest day of my life. I knew that losing someone who meant so much to me would change my world forever.

I talked to my father and aunt about the pain I experienced after my grandmother's death. We talked about my grief often. The conversations allowed me to express my thoughts and as a result, I was able to deal with the situation better than I would have if I was facing it alone. My aunt called and texted me regularly. She also sent spiritual messages from the Bible. My father talked me through several tough times. I relied on these two to pull me out of my darkest days. I'll never be able to thank them enough.

Fast forward several years to February of 2020. I moved back in with my father after selling my apartment. Although living with my father is a familiar experience, I'm still getting adjusted. I was used to having my own apartment. However, this is the right move for the moment. I'm living here while I wait to hear more about a police officer position I recently applied for. Once I complete the required academy, I will know where I will be assigned to work. My ultimate goal is to obtain a position in law enforcement then go back to school to earn a master's degree. I'd like to use that degree to obtain a teaching position. I'm passionate about imparting knowledge to the next generation of law enforcement officers.

CHAPTER FIVE

Life Lessons on Dealing with Adversity

NEVER GIVE UP

I have always known the importance of never giving up. We humans need hope — it's necessary to overcome the many obstacles life throws our way. Hope drives us to want things that are better and greater for ourselves, and it pushes us to make the necessary changes to achieve those things. When you rely on hope and believe that the possibilities are endless, you will find that God has already given you the energy and willpower necessary to keep on pushing.

My job at the railroad company serves as an example of never giving up. The job wasn't ideal from the start. I wasn't working in my chosen career field. Once I got hired,

I felt stuck. I knew I would have cleaning responsibilities, but I didn't realize how labor-intensive the position would be. I had never worked a cleaning job before, so I didn't know that I would hate this type of work. I dreaded going to work every day.

I knew I wanted to do more with my life. I knew that I *could* do more. I felt like the company was limiting my growth. Although it was frustrating, I didn't give up. I told myself that if this company would not allow me to advance to a new position, I would find one that did. I started applying for positions at other companies that aligned with my desired career path. As a result, I received job offers from agencies in my field. I'm in the process of exploring those opportunities as we speak.

WALK AWAY FROM TOXIC SITUATIONS

Whether it be a job or a relationship, we know when we're in a situation that is not healthy nor helping us grow. My railroad job also serves as an example of a toxic situation, primarily because it kept me stuck — there was no room to advance even though I had larger goals for myself. I was continually told that I failed the exams necessary to move up in the company. Those administering the exams never allowed me to see my scores — they simply told me that I didn't pass. I applied for managerial positions, which didn't carry the same exam requirements. Management positions required college degrees and experience. I met the requirements of the job postings time and time again. I was called for a few interviews; however, I wasn't selected for any of the open positions. The company put me in a box to stunt my potential. It was a toxic act, so I had to begin looking elsewhere for opportunities.

The same is true for several relationships I've had in my life. I've dated several women who behaved in ways that did not align with my values: women who constantly flirted with other men, who did not value hard work, and who simply wanted to use me rather than love me. In all of those cases, I knew that the temporary highs of feeling "in love" were not worth my long-term happiness. Again, these were toxic situations that I had to remove myself from, and my life has been all the better for doing so.

ASK FOR HELP

I was never ashamed to ask for help. I count that as one of the key reasons I've been able to overcome so many challenges in life. Sometimes people let their fear stop them from asking for help. It's the fear that keeps you from accomplishing your goals. It's the fear that stunts your growth. When you take a moment to think about it, you'll realize that your fear is often nothing more than irrational thinking. Essentially, irrational thinking is imagining a thought that is not logical or reasonable. It's irrational because, in most cases, you have no idea what others think of you. To find out what someone else is thinking, you have to ask that person. Even if you did ask that person, you have no way of verifying that what they say aligns with their true thoughts. As an example, let's say that I convince myself not to go to tutoring because I don't want people to think I'm stupid. This thought is irrational because I'm assuming people will think I'm stupid for seeking out tutoring, but I have no way of knowing that this is what people actually think. My point is, don't let what other people may or may not think of you stop you from accomplishing your goals.

I've had to ask for help on several occasions throughout my life. Remember that phone call I made to my grandmother on the night my mother came home intoxicated? I asked my grandmother for help. Once I reached out, support was given. If my grandmother didn't come to pick me up, I would have stayed in that terrible situation. One phone call made a difference. Some people don't ask for help even when they know that someone else can help them. That is how you know that your pride is getting in the way. I'm immensely grateful for my grandmother's help. It was her help that allowed me to finish high school and push myself further.

Another critical helper in my life has been my mentor. He helped me both academically and personally. When I was in college, I struggled with some of my courses. I called my mentor, told him I was having trouble, and he helped me. It's because of his help that I successfully passed my classes.

The help that I received never fell from the sky. In every instance, it started with an ask. Don't be afraid to ask for help. One of my favorite Bible verses highlights this message. It reads, "Ask, and it will be given to you; seek, and you will find; knock, and the door will be opened to you" (Matthew 7:7).

ACCEPT CHANGE AS PART OF THE PROCESS

Experiencing change is difficult, but it's necessary. To move forward in life, we must first accept that certain things will not remain the same. Life is unpredictable and the only constant is change. Often people are resistant to change because it requires effort and discipline. As people get older, people tend to want to do what they've been doing. They want to remain comfortable.

However, in many cases, what you've been doing may not be beneficial for you. It's important to recognize when that time comes and to start fresh if you need to. That might mean changing your living arrangement, your environment, or your relationships.

Let's look at an example of how change can be positive. When I moved back to New York to live with my grandmother, I dealt with change. It was hard. I left my mother and my sisters. I went to a high school that had a different ethnic makeup than I was used to. But ultimately, in South Carolina, I was living with an alcoholic, increasingly abusive mother. Relocating to New York benefited me greatly. It's the change that saved my life. I wouldn't be the man that I am today if I didn't accept that change is part of the process. The first step was to change my environment. It was hard but so necessary.

In conclusion, it's remarkable to be able to share my journey with you. I have a tremendous sense of accomplishment in being able to document my life story. It feels like giving a gift to the world. One of my favorite quotes comes from John Quincy Adams, who said, "If your actions inspire others to dream more, learn more, do more, become more, you are a leader." I certainly hope that my story has encouraged you to never give up when challenges come your way and to follow your dreams until you make them your reality.

www.ingramcontent.com/pod-product-compliance
Lightning Source LLC
Chambersburg PA
CBHW051714090426
42736CB00013B/2699